The Screw-Up's Guide to College

Inga Ambrosia

Copyright © 2020 Inga Ambrosia

All rights reserved.

ISBN: 978-0-9767224-0-3

DEDICATION

This book is dedicated to my students that are entering college, applying for college, entering high school, entering middle school, and still in elementary. I hope my time with you paved the way for a fantastic future.

"Effort only fully releases its reward after a person refuses to quit." – **Napoleon Hill**

The Screw-Up's Guide to College

CONTENTS

	Introduction	Pg 1
Chapter 1	Destination	Pg 3
2	Tuition	Pg 7
3	Requirements	Pg 9
4	Records & Recommendations	Pg 14
5	College Selection	Pg 15
6	Transportation/Commute	Pg 18
7	Cell Phone/Computers	Pg 20
8	College Success Plan	Pg 21
9	Expectations/Mentors	Pg 26
10	Clubs/Organizations	Pg 27
11	Career Choice	Pg 28
12	Job Market 101	Pg 32
13	Real Life 101	Pg 37
14	School Life	Pg 44
15	Personality Tweaks	Pg 46
	Checklist	Pg 49

"The successful warrior is the average man, with laser-like focus." - *Bruce Lee*

The Screw-Up's Guide to College

INTRODUCTION

This book isn't going to give you many answers. Think of it as a Scavenger Hunt. You'll find many questions, prompting you to do research to find your own version of truth. Each student reading this book will have a completely different journey, and a totally different path to get there. One Size Does Not Fit All. I know that because it took me 14 years to graduate college. I took the long road so you don't have to. I took my sweet time, playing around, partying, working, goofing off, and it cost me $500,000 dollars. I could have made $50,000 out of college, but instead, I wandered in the wilderness for 10 years, making minimum wage, or tips. I went to 3 different colleges, hoping that it was the building that needed to change ... not ME. I am grateful that I went back to college at 28 years old, because I was 16 when I arrived. Too clueless to know how clueless I really was.

When I returned, I had matured. I appreciated it more. Going to school is a privilege. I didn't take it for granted anymore. When I told employers that I didn't have a degree, I understood why doors were slammed in my face. When I held up my degree, I finally proved to myself that I could actually complete something difficult. A degree lets the world know, you're not a quitter. Are you better than someone who doesn't have one? They have their own journey. Many people never get a degree, and earn billions of dollars. If that's your path, have at it. If you want to go to college, and finish what you start, this is the book for you. You will repeatedly find questions that you think no one should be asking a kid. Too Bad. You're still going to have to know it. You might get frustrated when you can't find the answers easily. Too Bad. Life is tough, as my old boss used to say. I thought he was bitter. He was preparing me for the real world. Nothing worth doing comes easy. I am lucky to have awakened my "relentlessness", which is the key ingredient to becoming successful at anything. You have to have a kind of determination that makes no sense to anyone around you. You have to believe it before you see it, create your own reality by doing the work, and stepping into it.

This book is not calling you "A Screw Up". I was a Screw Up, and this is my guide to college. After a while, I just got tired of my own excuses. I got sick of listening to my own lies after a while. I wanted to walk away from my own silliness, but then I realize, I go – wherever – I go. These are the things you must face, and this is called maturity. Should you expect your parents to fill out everything and hold your hand? My parents didn't do that. Maybe they should have, but they didn't. If they did, I wouldn't be able to write this book. Again, I took the long road, and because of that I left you breadcrumbs along the way. Follow them, and you will meet me and others, that finished something we started, no matter what the cost, and can stand tall as:

<u>**COLLEGE GRADUATES**</u>

A Checklist is on the last page of this book. When you see this ☑ you may want to add it to the list.

1: DESTINATION

1) Name 5 colleges in your nearest big city:

   - _____
   - _____
   - _____
   - _____
   - _____

2) Do you want to go to college?   ___ yes
                                                                   ___ no

                                                                   _____ not sure

3) What do you want to study? _____
   _____
   _____

4) How many months/years will it take to achieve your degree/certificate? _____
   _____

5) Find 5 schools that offer your degree/certificate?

- _____
- _____
- _____
- _____
- _____

6) Did you know that if you go out of state, you could pay 3x the tuition? (Out of state fees) ___ yes
　　　　　　　　　　　　　　　　　　　　　　　　___ no

7) Have you seen your college's application form in paper or online?
　　　　　　　___ yes
　　　　　　　___ No (*You need to do that.) ☑

8) Do you know how the application process works?
　　　　　　　___ yes
　　　　　　　___ No (*You need to find out.) ☑

LIST THE PROCESS HERE:

- _____
- _____
- _____
- _____
- _____
- _____
- _____
- _____

9) How much is the application fee? _____
- _____
- _____
- _____
- _____
- _____
- _____
- _____
- _____

10) Do you know how to get that waived so you don't have to pay?

     ___ Yes
     ___ No (*You can do that.) ☑

11) What is the deadline to apply?

    _____ Spring
    _____ Summer
    _____ Fall

 * Deadlines are for people who wait until the last minute. You need to have your paperwork in early.

NOTE: Many college applications require essays and interviews. If you know you aren't good at writing an essay, you have time to ask someone to help you. ☑ Don't just "wing" it. Put your best foot forward. That's what the people at the top are doing. They aren't rolling the dice. They are stacking the deck, to make sure they win! Plan!

12) How will you pay for college?

        ____ Myself
        ____ Parents
        ____ Loans
        ____ Don't know

13) Do you have that money now?

        ____ Yes
        ____ No
        ____ Half
        ____ At least 1/3

14) Will you apply for scholarships?

        ____ Yes
        ____ No ☑

15) Which ones?

- _____
- _____
- _____
- _____

NOTE: Only students that apply for scholarships actually get them. Let that sink in. Put your hat in the ring, a lot! Submitting paperwork in extra early increases your changes.

2: TUITION

16) How much money are you seeking in scholarships?

_____

17) Have you applied for financial aid?

                     _____ Yes
                     _____ No ☑

18) Do you know how to apply for financial aid?

                     _____ Yes
                     _____ No
                     _____ A little

LIST THE PROCESS HERE:

- _____
- _____
- _____
- _____
- _____

19) What is the deadline to apply for financial aid?
_____

20) What is your Plan B if you don't get scholarships or financial aid? _____
_____
_____

21) Will your parents pay? How much will they contribute?
_____
_____

22) Do you keep a calendar of important dates/deadlines?
　　　____ Yes
　　　____ No ☑

* You must keep a daily, weekly, monthly, and yearly calendar if you want to succeed.

NOTE: If your parents don't have any money saved up for you for college, it's better to know that sooner rather than later. It's a terrible feeling to register for classes, get all the classes you want, and then have to go to the cashier, and be told your classes were dropped for nonpayment. Your parents may not tell you that they spent all your college money on the Nikes, PlayStation and IPhone that you asked for last Christmas. You'd better ask them for a college savings account before you request anymore "gifts". ☑

3: REQUIREMENTS

23) What is your current G.P.A.? _____

24) What G.P.A. is required for the colleges you want to attend? List them all.

- _____
- _____
- _____
- _____
- _____
- _____

25) Have you taken the SAT/ACT?
 ____ Yes
 ____ No ☑

You can take the SAT/ACT before 12th Grade.

26) Which test is preferred and which SAT/ACT Score is required for the colleges you want to attend?

- _____
- _____
- _____
- _____
- _____
- _____

27) Have you taken any practice tests online or in paper form for the SAT/ACT?

_____ Yes
_____ No ☑

28) Do you have a tutor to help you pass the SAT/ACT?

_____ Yes
_____ No

29) Do you know a SAT/ACT Preparation Course to help you pass the SAT/ACT?

_____ Yes
_____ No

30) How much is the course?

_____
_____
_____

The Screw-Up's Guide to College

31) When is the next course in your area or online?
_____

32) How much is a SAT/ACT Prep tutor?
_____

33) How will you pay for a tutor or a course?
_____

34) If you can't pay, what is your Plan B to prepare for SAT/ACT? _____
_____

35) Can you borrow an SAT/ACT Prep book from the library or buy one (even used)?
　　　　　　　　_____ Yes
　　　　　　　　_____ No ☑

36) What are the deadlines to take the SAT/ACT?
_____
_____

37) How much does the SAT or ACT cost in total?
_____
_____

38) Is there a way to get a waiver to take the test for free?
_____

39) How does taking the test multiple times affect your score? _____
_____

40) Which score will your college look at? _____

41) Do you know the other tests you need to take to enter college, and how some of your AP Advanced Placement courses will replace the need to take these tests? _____
_____
_____

NOTE: Taking Latin in middle school or high school will improve your understanding of root words and the meaning of words that you've never heard of. ☑ If it's available in your electives, take it. If you can get a book to study on your own, do it. Etymology is the study of the origin of words, especially polysyllabic (multiple syllables).

Many students trip over this portion, because they don't know how to break apart prefixes or suffixes, or how to dissect root words, to intelligently guess at big words. The greatest lesson that I learned in my SAT/ACT Prep course, was the ability to eliminate "stupid answers". Once you can reduce the choices, you increase your odds of choosing the right answer. Sometimes by 50%, basically a coin toss.

Also, familiarize yourself with the testing methodology. ☑ Do you get penalized for wrong answers? If not, never turn in a test with unanswered questions. Watch the time. Don't turn it into a panic attack, just pace yourself. Figure out how long you should spend on each question. If you don't know the answer, move on. Don't get stuck. A good tip before you take tests is to meditate to soft music to calm your nerves. Sleep well. Eat a green apple before.

42) Does your school offer Dual Enrollment, meaning you can go to high school and college at the same time?
   _____

43) Have you applied?

   _____ Yes
   _____ No
   _____ Enrolled ☑

44) What are the requirements?

   - _____
   - _____
   - _____
   - _____
   - _____

45) What are the benefits?

   - _____
   - _____
   - _____
   - _____
   - _____

NOTE: If you're the type of student that waits for your busy parents to fill out everything, you will miss the boat. Take them completed forms for them to sign. You mail it.

4: RECORDS & RECOMMENDATIONS

46) Do you know how to order transcripts ☑ (high school records) from your school's registrar? How much is it?
   _____

47) Do you know the address or college number (school code) to send them to? _____ Can it be done electronically? _____

48) Do you have 2 teachers that will give you a glowing recommendation letter? _____ Who are they?
   _____
   _____

49) Have you asked them already? _____
   _____ Yes
   _____ No ☑

   * If you don't have any teacher willing to give you one, you have to do some self-reflection. I had to go back to 9th and 10th grade. You don't want to have to beg.

5: COLLEGE SELECTION

50) What is the "graduation rate" of each college you want to attend? Compare the "retention rates", or who stays.

- _____
- _____
- _____
- _____
- _____
- _____

51) What are the demographics: race, gender, student, teachers, of the college you want to attend?

- _____
- _____
- _____
- _____
- _____
- _____

52) How many students are currently enrolled in total?

- _____
- _____
- _____
- _____
- _____
- _____

53) How many students are currently enrolled in your major at each school?

- _____
- _____
- _____
- _____
- _____

54) What is the cost of books per year at your college?

- _____
- _____
- _____
- _____
- _____
- _____

* Putting this on an Excel Spreadsheet will give you a full picture of how each school measures up. ☑

55) How much is room/board (dorms) at your college?

- _____
- _____
- _____
- _____
- _____

56) Will you live at home?

        ____ Yes
        ____ No

57) Will your family charge you rent?

        ____ Yes
        _____ How much?
        ____ No

58) Will you have a job? Where?
_____
_____

59) Will your job help you cover your expenses?

        ____ Yes
        ____ No

NOTE: Ask your parents what they expect from you as far as employment is concerned. ☑ If they want you to focus on school, will they be funding your expenses. How much?

6: TRANSPORTATION / COMMUTE

60) How will you get around? (Transportation)
_____

61) Will you pay for your own meals?
_____

62) Will you take the bus, Uber, Lyft?
_____

63) How much transportation to/from school per year?
_____
   Include plane tickets, trains, buses, gas, rideshare, rentals

64) What is the yearly budget for your own entertainment (movies, parties, shopping)? _____

65) Will you have a car? _____
    What kind? _____

66) Who will pay for the car? _____
    How much? _____

67) Who will pay for the insurance? _____
    How much yearly? _____

68) How much is total cost of having a car per month?

    _____ Gas
    _____ Maintenance
    _____ Insurance
    _____ Payments
    _____ Roadside Assistance

69) Who will pay for repairs? _____

    Repair Shop Name: _____

NOTE: You may not need a car. You spend less money when you don't have a car. You save money when you don't have a car. Never go out without cab fare, just in case your friends want to start acting shady, you can find your own way home. When you go to school in the city, you spend less on travel. Family is closer if you need help. Homesickness is a #1 reason why students that go to school out of state return home after the first year, #2 is heartbreak.

Students tend to get buck wild when they leave home too soon. Don't assume you are one of the lucky ones that won't. The more sheltered you are, the more likely you will become hypnotized by the foolishness surrounding college campus. Immature people flunk out of college every day.

7: CELL PHONE / COMPUTERS

70) Will you have a cell phone?
　　　　　　　____ Yes
　　　　　　　____ No

71) Who will pay for the cell phone? _____
　　 How much monthly? _____

72) Will you have a laptop?
　　　　　　　____ Yes
　　　　　　　____ No

73) Who will pay for the laptop? _____
What kind and How much? _____

NOTE: You don't need a fancy phone. The less apps you have on your phone, the better you'll do in school. If you find yourself spending hours on social media, texting, watching videos, please know you're taking money out of your future self's bank account. Get a cheap phone or none. Don't give out your number. Less calls = Less distraction.

8: COLLEGE SUCCESS PLAN

74) Who will you study with at college? _____

75) How many classes will you take per semester?
_____

76) Will you take morning, afternoon, night classes or a mixture? _____

77) Will you go part-time or full-time?
_____

78) How much longer to graduate if you go part-time?
_____

79) What is an Academic Warning? _____
_____
_____

80) What is Academic Probation? _____
_____
_____

81) What is an Academic Dismissal? _____
_____
_____

82) How many hours a day will you study? _____

83) How many hours a day do you study now? _____

84) Do you believe you have to study more or less in college? _____

85) Are you a self-starter or do you procrastinate?
_____

86) Do you cram (the night before) for exams or do you study all week long? _____

87) Do you start projects immediately or wait until the last minute? _____

88) Do you read ahead in the chapter before you get to class or wait for the teacher to spoon feed you? _____
_____

89) Do you ask questions in class or do you just listen? ___
_____

90) Will you skip class? _____

91) How will you get your notes if you miss class?
_____
_____

92) How will you take notes in class? Paper, Computer, Recorder etc. _____

93) Will you rewrite, type, or put your notes on note cards to further solidify the information in your mind? _____
_____

What I Did Earlier: I would go to class and just show my face. I took notes, but I never looked at them when I left class. My handwriting is terrible. I could barely read what I wrote later. Notes were irrelevant because I didn't read the text beforehand. It didn't get saturated into my mind.

What I Did 10 Years Later: I read the text before I went to class. I took notes then. When I went to class, I took more notes from the lecture to supplement my own handwritten notes. Then, when I went home, I typed up my notes on a computer. Printed them out. Made note cards out of those notes. Went online to find out additional information about the topic so I stayed interested. I didn't just eat what the professor gave me. I went out and found my own extra details. If it's not interesting, I'm probably not going to remember it. I love finding out rare facts that even the professor doesn't know. It keeps me engaged.

I also would watch a documentary, a movie, a video clip, read journals, articles, listen to audio clips of whatever topic we were discussing. My brain can hold a lot of information. Yours can too. If you don't give it something to do, it will find a way to fill itself up, i.e. Reality T.V., gossip, nonsense.

NOTE: Past behavior is a good indicator of future behavior. If you're lackluster in high school, you are probably going to continue the same behavior with less structure. Professors don't care if you show up, they still get paid. They don't care if you pass the class, their checks are the same. They will not chase you to do homework. They may not even check it. Many assignments are voluntary, making quizzes, tests, and papers the weight of your grade. If you don't have discipline, you'll be on your own. Don't take online classes if you can't stay motivated.

Students that need their teachers to beg them to do homework, call their parents, or beg them to pay attention in class, will be in for a rude awakening, when the professor won't even know your name. I served one of my professors at a restaurant I worked at in college. She didn't even recognize me. I was just a student number. Some classes have more than 300 students in them. I had one class that was in an auditorium. My professor emerged from the curtain, taught her lesson, and disappeared behind the curtain. She didn't take questions, and she didn't slow down. It was a PowerPoint Bonanza. I had to take that class twice.

First day of school, sit in the front row. The person on the left of you and the right of you are your study partners. Get their schedule, and pick a study time every day or every other day. Be on time. Do your part. People that sit in the back of the room, want to be away from the teacher. People in the front row are usually overachievers. That's your network. Let the professor know who you are by going to their office hours, otherwise, you are not memorable. Let them know you are trying to get an 'A' in this class. Don't be arrogant, just let them know in a humble, sweet way.

After every assignment, go get clarification of what they want. Write a paper in advance, let them look over it. If they make a change, guess what, they just wrote your paper. They can't mark it wrong. Never ever cheat on tests, papers, or assignments. You can get expelled, and no you won't get your money back. Just do things the right way, and you will be ahead of everyone that's looking for a shortcut. Sacrifice social time. You have more fun in your 20s when you actually have a job, money, and some common sense.

Don't do things you will regret like getting tattoos, piercings, or altering your body. You will be wearing your mistakes for the rest of your life. Just wait until you mature fully. Don't try to go to the college all your friends go to either. Unless you all are top students, serious about making it to the top, they will just slow you down. It will be a continuation of high school. You will meet some of the most amazing people in college. People you could possibly start businesses with. It will be a whole new set of people. Be open to the idea of expanding your network.

Let me also recommend that you seriously consider a career in technology. There are so many jobs that you are considering that will be obsolete by the time you graduate. I do a lot of career fairs, classes, career days, workshops, where I tell young kids that most of the jobs you see today will be eliminated by a robot, Artificial Intelligence, Smart technology etc. It's not a joke. You will either be fixing the robot, programming it, designing it, or being replaced by it. This is not something that is far off. This is right around the corner. Before you choose a career. Take a look if you are setting yourself up for failure. You heard it here first. The future is here, and technology will automate everything soon. Look into Engineering, Robotics, AI, Automation, STEM.

9: EXPECTATIONS/MENTORS

94) Do you know anyone who finished college? Who? ____
_____
_____

95) Interview them about their college journey? Be Bold! Their story: _____
_____
_____
_____
_____
_____
_____
_____
_____
_____

NOTE: Take whatever they say with a grain of salt. Their experience may be totally different from yours. There will be similarities. Ask a few people for advice. Make sure you ask people that you trust, not party animals or silly folks.

10: CLUBS / ORGANIZATIONS

96) Will you pledge in a fraternity or sorority?
 _____ Yes
 _____ No

97) What ways can hazing go terribly wrong? _____
_____

98) Will you play a sport? _____
 Which one(s)? _____
_____

99) Which clubs/organizations will you join? _____
_____
_____

NOTE: Joining organizations is fine, as long as it doesn't interfere with your studies. It looks good on a resume if you are in a club, even better if you hold an office in a club. Joining organizations just for the mixers and party aspect is a complete waste of time. Make your activities count towards your future goals, otherwise skip them altogether.

11: CAREER CHOICE

100) Which books have you read on your career?

- _____
- _____
- _____
- _____
- _____

101) Name 4 people you know personally that are in your career. Where did they graduate from?

1. _____
_____
2. _____
_____
3. _____
_____
4. _____
_____

102) Research 4 people you don't know who have your career. Search LinkedIn or company websites.

1. _____
2. _____
3. _____
4. _____

103) Name 3 places you can work after you graduate.

1. _____
2. _____
3. _____

104) What internships are offered for your career?

_____
_____

105) Contact any of the 3 places you can work in your area to see if you can intern now? ☑ What is the result?

_____

106) What is the starting annual salary of your career?

_____

107) What is the highest position you can have in your career? _____

108) What do you need to obtain that position? An advanced degree, such as Masters, Ph.D., Psy.D., Specialization, or extra certificate training? _____
_____
_____

109) How much does the extra education or training cost?
_____
_____

110) Which colleges that you chose offer this special training? _____
_____
_____

111) Which ones offer a combined Bachelors / Masters / Ph.D. program? What is required to be admitted?
_____
_____
_____

NOTE: The number of graduates that seek advanced Master's degrees is miniscule compared to undergraduates overall. Once you look at Ph.D. graduate numbers, it's too small to see even with a microscope. The reason is, people don't think about their college career in the long term. If you goof off as a freshman, that will hurt you when it's time to be accepted into graduate school. Check out the requirements for graduate school now for your degree. ☑

REQUIREMENTS FOR Master's Degree:

- _____
- _____
- _____
- _____
- _____
- _____

REQUIREMENTS FOR Ph.D., Psy.D., J.D. etc:

- _____
- _____
- _____
- _____
- _____
- _____

NOTE: Looking at the requirements when you're already in your last year of undergrad is a little late. You have to look at that map before you ever embark on the journey of Higher Education. People with advanced degrees tend to make more money, and are starting in higher positions sooner than regular Bachelor's Degree undergraduates. Graduate school costs money. Either you'll have loans or scholarships. There are ways to pay for graduate school that only those who seek will find. There are fellowships, faculty-recommended scholarships, employers that will pay for the whole thing or reimburse you etc. Starbucks gives employees full scholarships. Do a quick search of companies today, and you'll be 4+ years ahead. ☑

12: JOB MARKET 101

112) Look at Indeed, Monster, Ziprecruiter, or the newspaper classifieds, for openings to see what your future job is requiring right now? Print the listings. ☑

REQUIREMENTS FOR Current Job Openings:

- _____
- _____
- _____
- _____
- _____

113) Look at company websites that you think you could work for, read their current openings and job descriptions. Print them and compare. ☑ ____ Done

114) Which college would prepare you the most for this job if you graduated today? _____

115) What kind of prior work experience is required?
_____

116) Have you ever had a job interview?
　　　　　____ Yes
　　　　　____ No

117) What is the title(s) of the person(s) who will interview you for your career job?
_____
_____
_____

118) Do you know what is inappropriate to wear to an interview? _____
_____
_____

119) Go online and find what you think is appropriate. Print it. Ask someone in Human Resources at your school if this is appropriate for your career. Include pictures of shoes. ☑　　　　　　　____ Done

120) Ask someone in your career field if they think this is good for an interview.　　　　　　　____ Done

121) What makeup, hairstyle, haircut, hair dye, nails, jewelry is considered **not** appropriate for the interview or the job? _____
_____
_____

NOTE: Some interviewers know they aren't going to hire you immediately, based on the way you dress and present yourself. Know before you go, it's a game. You have to act like you know the rules, or you don't play.

122) Currently, what is on your social media that is inappropriate for someone in the career? Remove it today. ☑ _____

_____

_____

*Inappropriate pictures, themes, captions or statements will come back to bite you later on. Employers search web crawlers looking for all instances of an applicant's name, email, handle, and phone number.

123) What things have you said in the past that a future employer will find if they dig deep enough? _____

_____

_____

*I remember a Ph.D. candidate, applying for a job with me as a teacher. I looked up his email address, and found a Facebook account with music he'd made, filled with curse words, slurs, and very bizarre pictures of him posing with his friends. He was only a freshman back then. He never removed it, and left it for me to find.

124) Is your email address inappropriate or does it include your real name or a nickname? _____

125) Find a sample cover letter online. ☑   ____ Done

126) Write one of your own and have someone in your field read it. Your first one will be awful. ____ Done

*Rewrite it regularly as you go through school and college so it's perfect later. Use multiple relevant samples.

127) What kind of references do you need for the interview? _____
_____
_____

*Be careful using your "rough around the edges" friends as references. If they have foul music as their music on hold, or voicemail, you could be screwed. Also, don't use family that will overshare, and do more harm than good. Please, don't use a job as a reference when you know you didn't leave there on good terms.

128) How will you get these references, especially if they need to be on letterhead? _____
_____

129) What are the professional associations, groups or organizations you can join for your career? _____
_____
_____

130) Are the organizations local, regional, national, or worldwide? _____

131) What is the cost to join these organization as a student now? _____

132) What are the opportunities for mentorship or scholarships available to you while in college?
_____
_____
_____

133) Name the career fairs or job fairs for your career in your area? _____
_____
_____
_____

134) When is the next one in your area, and who do you see that might be in your career there? _____
_____
_____

* Go to one, even at your age, just to ask questions. ☑ If anyone tries to talk you out of going, saying it's too early, and that you don't even have a resume, ignore them. People are very intimidated by fast-moving, overachieving, forward-thinking, ahead-of-the-curve type people. You might as well get used to that resistance. Stay the course!

135) How much does it cost to attend the fair? How will you get there? _____
_____
_____
_____

NOTE: Ask loads of questions. Walk right up to the table Bold As Ever. Tell them that you want to speak with someone about an internship or possible job. Shake their hand, look them in the eye, and take a card. Follow up! Email them immediately when you get home. Remind them of who you are. Call them in a week. Be brave. ☑

13: REAL LIFE 101

136) What is the starting monthly salary for your career? (Divide annual salary by 12) _____

*Keep a calculator handy so you can fill in the following:

137) What kind of apt. or house could you afford if you worked in your career today? Look on Zillow or Realtor or HotPads. Look for what you want first.
_____
_____

138) What is your monthly payment? _____
Multiply this number X 3 _____ (3:1 ratio)

*You need to be able to pay your rent 3 times with your salary. Your payment must be 1/3 of your monthly salary. If rent is $1,100, you need to make $3,300/mo.

139) Can you afford what you want? _____
_____ Yes
_____ No
_____ Lol

140) Subtract your payment from your monthly salary.
_____ = New Monthly Salary

**Create an Excel spreadsheet and a new column called New Monthly Salary. Every time we have an expense, subtract it from there. ☑

141) Are you willing to have a roommate or downsize to save money?

____ Yes
____ No

142) How much would furniture cost? Look up Ashley Furniture or Rooms To Go, and pick your bedroom, living room, dining room sets. How much?

Bedroom Set _____
Living Room Set _____
Dining Room Set _____
TOTAL: _____

143) Go to Bed Bath and Beyond, Walmart, or Ikea and pick your kitchenware and bathroom accessories.

Kitchenware _____
Bathroom Set _____
Decorations _____
TOTAL: _____

144) Can you afford all of that on the current monthly salary for your job? _____

145) Are you willing to buy used furniture or shop garage sales to save money, or to go without luxuries until you can afford it?

     ____ Yes
     ____ No

NOTE: You don't need to impress anyone. If you don't have nice stuff, don't invite people over. Period.

146) Will you put anything on credit cards?

     ____ Yes
     ____ No

147) What is the average interest rate on a credit card?
_____

148) What is a credit score? _____
_____
_____

149) What is an: Excellent credit score? _____
       Average credit score? _____
       Poor credit score? _____

150) Ask your parents what their credit score is.
_____

 *They can order their credit score on Credit Karma, or call the 3 credit agencies to have it mailed to them. Experian, TransUnion and Equifax. Ask them how they got that credit score. _____
_____
_____

151) Ask them how it has affected them, good or bad.
_____
_____
_____
_____
_____

152) Which designer clothes will you purchase when you are in your career? _____
_____
_____

153) How much will you spend on designer clothes or shoes per month? _____

154) Write a column, if you're taking notes, or using Excel called Not Saved. Include this number from your designer budget (above). ☑   ____ Done

155) Subtract the above number from your monthly salary _____ = New Monthly Salary.

156) Will you pay cash or will you use credit cards for your clothes/shoes budget? _____

157) Will you pay the credit card off every month? _____ If not, please add 18% to 22% to the amount of your clothes and shoes. This is the number you will overpay for your items. Think of it as the opposite of a discount. You will be overpaying.

158) Will you ever pay a late? _____ If so, please add $25 late fee. Don't pay bills LATE!

NOTE: Most teenagers get credit card applications in the mail immediately upon turning 18. Never open them. Shred them and save yourself thousands of dollars.

159) What is the annual fee on 3 different credit cards? Do your research. Divide this number by 12, this is how much of a fee you will pay every month.

    1. _____
    2. _____
    3. _____

160) Will you eat at restaurants? _____
    How often per month? _____
    What is the total spent on restaurants? _____
    Subtract this from your monthly salary = _____
    Add it to column Not Saved = _____

161) What dinners can you make at home for less?
_____

162) What is the price of a cookbook? _____

163) Ask your parents what their monthly bills cost: ☑

    Water Bill: _____
    Cable Bill: _____
    Electric Bill: _____

NOTE: Granted, you may not be living in the same type of house. You don't want your first time seeing a bill to be when you have to pay it as an adult. It can be shocking.

164) Find someone who has the house you want and ask them the amount of those same bills. Keep asking until you find someone.

Water Bill: _____
Cable Bill: _____
Electric Bill: _____

165) Add all of these bills up, then subtract them from your New Monthly Salary. _____

166) Are you in the red yet, meaning, did you spend more than you earn? What is the balance? _____

167) Would you be willing to get a second job to maintain your lifestyle? _____ Where would you work? __
_____

168) Find out the average student loan debt for your college? _____

169) Divide this number by 10 years, and then by 12 months. This is your monthly payment. Subtract this number from your New Monthly Salary.
_____

NOTE: Most students carry student loan debt.

170) What are the federal or states taxes you will pay on your salary in percentage? _____

171) Divide this number by 12. This is what you will pay each month. Subtract this number from your New Monthly Salary. _____

172) Do you still believe this is the career choice for you? Why or Why Not? _____
_____
_____
_____

173) Would you be willing to relocate for your job to earn more money?
                 _____ Yes
                 _____ No

174) Would you consider moving to another country for your job? Which country? _____

175) Are your parents supportive of your career choice?
_____

176) Are you willing to pursue your career choice even if they don't support you? _____

NOTE: In some cultures, parents don't support their kids' career choices, and they withhold funding and moral support. You have to be willing to forge ahead, even if you feel that you'll be going it alone. You'll only get stronger once you realize, you will end up living your choices on your own anyways. It's better to be happy with what you're doing. If your career choice makes the world a better place, then you have all the approval you need! My dad wanted me to be a lawyer, I chose Psychology. He got over it.

14: SCHOOL LIFE

177) Do you like school? Why or Why Not? _____
_____
_____

178) Which subject do you like the most and why? _____
_____
_____

179) What experiences in school have effected your self-esteem? _____
_____
_____

180) Have you ever been bullied for your career choice?
_____
_____

181) What steps are you taking to improve your self-esteem? _____
_____
_____

182) How do you challenge yourself in school to build confidence? _____
_____

183) What leadership roles do you have in school? _____
_____
_____

184) What books do you read for fun? _____
_____
_____
_____

185) Do you have a lot of friends or are you a loner?
_____

186) If you lose friends will you still complete your goals?
_____
_____

187) How do you feel being alone? _____
_____
_____

188) Do you find yourself needing constant approval from others? _____
_____

NOTE: Lao Tzu, an ancient philosopher once stated in a book, "Care about what other people think, and you will be their prisoner." School is a training ground for adulthood, don't get stuck in the halls and walls. All of it is temporary.

15: PERSONALITY TWEAKS

189) How do you follow up if you don't hear back from people? _____
_____
_____

190) What is the difference between being assertive vs. aggressive? _____
_____
_____

191) What is the difference between being persistent vs. being a pest? _____
_____
_____

192) What does "out of sight, out of mind?" mean? _____
_____
_____

*The person that speaks up, is the person that eats. If you stay quiet, you will be passed over. Adults forget things. Don't take it personal, just remind them and keep asking.

193) Are you relentless (unstoppable) or do you give up easily when you don't find what you need?
_____

194) Are successful people relentless or do they give up easily? _____

195) Do you face your fears or do you run from them?
_____
_____

196) How do you resolve fears that you don't face? _____
_____
_____

197) How successful do you think you'll be in your career? _____
_____
_____
_____

198) What is your greatest fear regarding your career?
_____
_____
_____

NOTE: Fear of Success and Fear of Failure are identical. Some people never try because they are afraid to fail. Some people never try because they are afraid to succeed. Both are afraid of success, because failure may follow in their minds. Some people are afraid of regret, so they try harder.

199) What qualities do you have that could make you successful? _____
_____
_____
_____
_____

200) What parts of your personality could prevent you from being successful? _____
_____
_____
_____

201) How willing are you to change the parts of your personality that prevent you from being successful?
_____
_____

202) Do you have your own mind or do you follow the crowd, even if they are dead wrong? _____
_____

203) Would you rather lose play time or lose sleep for your goal? _____
_____

204) What are some things that make you happy? _____
_____
_____
_____

205) Are you ready for college? If you filled out this entire book, read it over with your friends and family, checked with your teachers and mentors, then **YES**! Pass it on!

CHECKLIST

DATE	THING TO DO	DUE DATE	DONE ☑

ABOUT THE AUTHOR

Inga Ambrosia is an educator, business owner, Life Coach, and a philosophical writer. She has written many books on biochemistry, psychology, metaphysics, and quantum physics. She lives in South Florida, and has been a vegan for 16 years.

HER OTHER BOOKS:

God's Pharmacy Book Series (Adult Nonfiction)

TOUR / WORKSHOPS / LECTURES:

She is available for speaking engagements:
Contact: inga@godspharmacybook.com

www.ingramcontent.com/pod-product-compliance
Lightning Source LLC
Chambersburg PA
CBHW020811160426

43192CB00006B/523